The Struggling Disciple

THE STRUGGLING DISCIPLE

Meditations on Peter, the Fisherman

Richard L. Rustad

COLLINS

Cleveland • New York

Published by William Collins Publishers, Inc.
Cleveland • New York

Scripture quotations in this publication are from the Revised Standard Version Common Bible copyrighted ©1973 by the Division of Christian Education of the National Council of the Churches of Christ and are used by permission.

First published 1979

COPYRIGHT © 1979 BY RICHARD L. RUSTAD

All rights reserved. No part of this publication may be reproduced, stored in a retrieval system, or transmitted in any form or by any means, electronic, mechanical, photocopying, or otherwise, without the prior permission of the publisher.

Library of Congress Cataloging in Publication Data
Rustad, Richard L.
  The struggling disciple.
  1. Peter, Saint, apostle—Meditations. I. Title.
BS2515.R87   225.9'24   79-16992
ISBN 0-529-05670-4

Printed in the United States of America

The Struggling Disciple

To my wife, Sandy
and children, Carrie and Eric

Contents

Foreword   11

1. Follow Me   15

2. Conquering Our
   Contradictions   23

3. Twice As Many
   Ears   29

4. Construction Kits   37

5. Shedding Skins   45

6. The Resurrection
   of Peter   53

7. I Believe Jesus
   Goes On Before   61

8. One Who Notices   69

9. God Has No
   Favorites   77

10. One Street Farther   85

Foreword

At the midpoint of my life, there came a sense of urgency to leave behind unwanted parts of myself. As I was launched forth on this journey to find my real self, to find a new honesty about myself with others, Peter's life, his journey, provided a road map. As the reality of his life unfolded, the essence of my own life began to develop in exciting ways.

As my search intensified, there began to emerge a picture of Peter as a person with whom we can identify as we seek to respond to Christ's summons to discipleship.

This book represents nuggets of an encounter that I have had with Peter and, as a result, with Jesus Christ and myself. That has brought new richness, new openness, new purpose, and new meaning to my life. It is hoped that this sharing with you may galvanize you to embark on such an adventure yourself.

The Bible passages preceeding each of the meditations serve as the background for the thoughts on Peter that follow. The Scripture passages are from the Revised Standard Version of the Bible, but you will find that there are occasions throughout when I have chosen to use quotations either from the New English Bible (NEB) or William Barclay's translation of the New Testament.

There are many who have been of support in my spiritual pilgrimage, especially my family and close friends. I am indebted to them for their love and steadfast help.

I wish also to acknowledge the work of my secretaries, Joyce Moenich and Patricia Berlo, and the helpful suggestions by Sharon Ringe when reviewing the initial manuscript.

Lent 1979

Richard L. Rustad

Matthew 4:18–22

As *Jesus* walked by the Sea of Galilee, he saw two brothers, Simon who is called Peter and Andrew his brother, casting a net into the sea; for they were fishermen. And he said to them, "Follow me, and I will make you fishers of men." Immediately they left their nets and followed him. And going on from there he saw two other brothers, James the son of Zeb'edee and John his brother, in the boat with Zeb'edee their father, mending their nets, and he called them. Immediately they left the boat and their father, and followed him.

1

Follow Me

The Call

As *Jesus* walked by the Sea of Galilee, he saw two brothers, Simon who is called Peter and Andrew his brother, casting a net into the sea; for they were fishermen. And he said to them, "Follow me, and I will make you fishers of men." Immediately they left their nets and followed him.

In all its simplicity, this scene has powerful implications. It presents the call to us to be followers of Christ. As you read this passage, allow yourself also to *hear* the gospel in such a way that it may reach the core of your life. Only as you do, will you grasp that the call of the risen Lord is not something locked in the history of long ago. It is a call you can experience if you but hear the good news, feel the presence of Christ, and respond to his invitation to follow him. And if you do, there is Easter and your own ressurrection is at hand.

Peter and Andrew were fishermen. Do you suppose that our Lord chose them because of that? Do you figure that he chose them because fishermen make natural evangelists? I think the answer is "No." They had no special qualifications, no special training or aptitude. They were as ordinary as you or I. We are never chosen because of what we are, but because of what God is like. We can't take this passage seriously and still carry on with our worn-out excuses about not being trained or qualified or worthy to do this thing or that in the church. Peter and Andrew had no special qualifications.

They were also very busy. They weren't just loafing around looking for something to do. They were hard at work when Christ called them. They left their nets and followed him. You are always going to have to leave something behind if you are going to follow Jesus Christ. If you don't leave it behind, you can't make room for what could take its place.

When we first think of Peter and Andrew leaving their nets and following Jesus, we might get the picture that what was involved was changing their location, changing their occupation. To follow Christ doesn't mean that at all. It is not a matter of changing your place of residence or your work, but of changing your loyalties. You can stay right where you are, in the same house, the same job, but your loyalties have to be given over to God.

Christ used a remarkable play on words when he called the fishermen to be fishers of men. It was especially fitting for the way in which he called Peter and Andrew. To be a fisher of men means that you are willing to be a servant of God. "Will you stop fishing for yourself and fish for me?" was the question. They answered, "Yes." What will your answer be to the call to be a follower of the Lord Jesus Christ?

Norman Cousins begins his book on Albert Schweitzer by describing the regular after-dinner ritual which prevailed in the jungle hospital in Lambarene. The great doctor announced the hymn to be sung and walked over to an old dilapidated piano on the other side of the room. Cousins says that the piano must have been at least fifty years old. The keyboard was badly stained. Several screws fastened the ivory to the keys, and quite a few important strings were missing. Under equatorial conditions of extreme heat and moisture, the piano was badly out of tune. Now, one of the world's great musicians and a renowned interpreter of Bach's music, sat down to play. The amazing and wondrous thing, Cousins goes on to say, was that the piano seemed to "lose its poverty in his hands." Its tinniness and clattering echoes seemed subdued. The missing and out-of-tune notes seemed to give way to a beauty that moments ago seemed impossible. Its capacity to yield music was now being fully realized (Norman Cousins, *Dr. Schweitzer at Lambarene* [New York: Harper & Brothers, 1960], pp. 9-10).

That piano is much like we are. Our Master accepts us with all our faults, and as long as we are sensitive to his touch brings out the best that is within us. Our lives are stained with sin. We have all kinds of shortcomings and have made lots of mistakes. If we but hear the call of Christ and wholeheartedly respond to the touch of the Master, there will be music, there will be love, there will be joy. The poverty of our life will fade away and there will come a peace, a sense of meaning and purpose, a sense of fulfillment that has before seemed impossible.

Return to the Nets

It would be nice if this was the end of Peter's and Andrew's story. You can't end it there and be honest. You can't end the story with the disciples hearing Jesus' call and gladly responding. There is more to their story than that. After Jesus' death, Peter along with Thomas and Nathanael, went back to the sea, back to their boats, back to fishing again. They fished all night and caught nothing. Jesus appeared to them on the shore and told them where to cast their net. They did as he suggested and their net was so full of fish that they could not haul it aboard. You remember how Peter swam to the shore. You remember how Jesus told Peter to feed his sheep. It was the same call to discipleship all over again that they needed to rehear.

The point is not that they had returned to the Sea of Galilee again. The point is not that they had gone back to their old occupation any more than their original calling meant to leave the sea and their fishing. The point is that, like Peter, we are always going back fishing, like him we have to rehear the old call "Follow me" and respond anew. We are never done with repentance once and for all. However many times we have left our nets, we go back fishing again and have to hear the calling once more.

Remember the story told by Mother Goose:

"Pussy cat, pussy cat, where have you been?

I've been to London to visit the queen.
Pussy cat, pussy cat, what did you there?
I frightened a little mouse under her chair."

For a cat to go to London would really be something. To go there to visit the Queen—that is a monumental event. What happened when pussy cat got there? She completely lost sight of the mission she was on, reverted to her lower nature, and did nothing but frighten a little mouse under her chair.

We are like that. We feel moments of calling and inspiration, times when we have let God touch us. In those moments, we have all kinds of ideas about what we are going to do for God and the church of Jesus Christ. But all too often, we just end up chasing mice. We lose touch with God. We lose touch with what he is calling us to do as his servants. In the process, we lose touch with ourselves.

The Real Resurrection

Peter left his fishing to be a fisher of persons. Then, he went back to fishing again. It was when he was back at the nets again that he saw Christ on the shore. Christ told him to feed his sheep. Jesus indicated the manner in which Peter would die and added, "Follow me." Then, Peter asked about what would happen to John and Jesus said, "If it should be my will that he wait until I come, what is it to you?" He added, again, "Follow me."

Peter needed to hear that basic summons to discipleship over and over again: "Follow me." The same Christ is with us today, speaking the summons of old: "Follow me, and I will make you fishers of men."

The saving power which transformed a simple fisherman, who was impulsive, often short-sighted, and sometimes lacking in courage into the servant of Christ who took the task upon his shoulders to be the leader of the newborn church, that same power which transformed him can transform us as well.

Dr. Carl Marlett, who wrote the familiar hymn "Are Ye Able," tells a parable of salvation that took place years ago on the Irish Sea.

Dr. Marlett was stage manager once of the Chautauqua productions at Rushville, Indiana. There he heard a concert by the Royal Welsh Male Quartette. The program was of light, popular music until the last number when the mood suddenly changed. Dr. Marlett sensed in the singers a deep emotion. Later, he mentioned that to them. They were at first reluctant to tell their story, but then it came out.

They were on the Lusitania when it was torpedoed and 1,153 persons drowned. When it looked like the ship was going down for sure, they decided to give up their lifebelts to women and children. So they dove out into the water together, resolved to help each other as long as they could keep going.

The darkness came and the cold. Their power to keep holding on to the wreckage of the ship was waning. Whenever someone couldn't keep going, the others held him up until his strength returned. Finally, they thought that they were all at the end of the rope. They decided that since they had lived singing, that they would die singing. So their voices sounded over the turbulent sea:

> "Jesus, lover of my soul,
> Let me to thy bosom fly,
> While the nearer waters roll,
> While the tempest still is high;
> Hide me, O my Savior, hide,
> Till the storm of life is past;
> Safe into the haven guide;
> O receive my soul at last!"

A rescue crew from a destroyer was straining their eyes and ears in the howling wind. They heard that song faintly coming out of the storm and headed in that direction.

> "Other refuge have I none;
> Hangs my helpless soul on thee
>   Leave, ah! leave me not alone
>   Still support and comfort me.
> All my trust on thee is stayed;
> All my help from thee I bring;

> Cover my defenseless head
> With the shadow of thy wing."

In the night they found the men, specks in the towering waves. When they finally got them back to the destroyer, there was a great cheer. The four men stood on the deck, safe at last, and with their arms around each other, finished the song, the great hymn of Charles Wesley:

> "Plenteous grace with thee is found,
> Grace to cover all my sin;
> Let the healing streams abound;
> Make and keep me pure within.
> Thou of life the fountain art;
> Freely let me take of thee:
> Spring thou up within my heart;
> Rise to all eternity."

The more I have thought of that story, the more I have realized that the real moment of salvation took place, not when they were hoisted aboard the ship but when they gave their lifebelts away. The essence of Easter in their story is not the fact that they lived to tell it, but that they had learned to die to self.

The call is an old one but ever new: "Follow me."

Luke 5:1–11

While the people pressed upon him to hear the word of God, he was standing by the lake of Gennesaret. And he saw two boats by the lake; but the fishermen had gone out of them and were washing their nets. Getting into one of the boats, which was Simon's, he asked him to put out a little from the land. And he sat down and taught the people from the boat. And when he had ceased speaking, he said to Simon, "Put out into the deep and let down your nets for a catch." And Simon answered, "Master, we toiled all night and took nothing! But at your word I will let down the nets." And when they had done this, they enclosed a great shoal of fish; and as their nets were breaking, they beckoned to their partners in the other boat to come and help them. And they came and filled both the boats, so that they began to sink. But when Simon Peter saw it, he fell down at Jesus' knees, saying, "Depart from me, for I am a sinful man, O Lord." For he was astonished, and all that were with him, at the catch of fish which they had taken; and so also were James and John, sons of Zeb'edee, who were partners with Simon. And Jesus said to Simon, "Do not be afraid; henceforth you will be catching men." And when they had brought their boats to land, they left everything and followed him.

2

Conquering Our Contradictions

When I was teaching counseling technique to pastors and priests in the master's degree program at Cleveland Psychiatric Institute, one of the pet phrases that I used so often as to bring a smile the next time was this: "Tack down the ambivalence." It is important to help persons clarify the struggle that they are going through. Often, we want to do something and don't want to do it at the same time. Things don't come to us as clear-cut issues. If everything was that clear, that black and white, we wouldn't need to go to a pastor or friend to sort things out. Many times we have an intellectual answer and an emotional answer to the same question and the answers are different. Our struggle may be whether to listen to our head or to our heart. It is only when this is recognized that the ambivalence is tacked down, and it is then that we can begin to make creative judgments about our lives.

For the past two years, I have been fascinated by the person of Peter in the New Testament. I am just beginning to understand why that is so. Peter is fascinating because we can see in him the paradoxes that we are slow to acknowledge in ourselves. Maybe in looking at him we can gain enough courage to take another honest look at ourselves.

When we think of examples, we usually think of good or bad ones. That tends to be artificial at best. Peter is both together, and that is why he is such an appealing figure. He is a true example of believers, his life, in other words, is typical of one who believes in Christ. He is representative of the church. We see in him faith and denial, potential and failure, a present self and a possible self. When we look at Peter, we can have a feeling of a sense of journey. He comes through all these contradictions within himself to resurrection. Even his failure is important. Each time he failed, it provided Jesus the opportunity to teach, to show the way to eternal life. It helps us to realize that God can use not only our strengths, but even our failures if our lives are committed to him. Let us see how this unfolds in the Scripture passage you have just read.

The Point

Peter and the others had been fishing all night without success. Morning came and they went ashore exhausted with nothing much to show for their efforts other than nets that had to be washed. That wouldn't have been so difficult if their fishing that night had been fruitful, but cleaning the nets would have been sheer drudgery in the light of their failure. Jesus got into Peter's boat and asked him if he would put out from shore a ways and he began to teach the people from the prow of the boat. He then asked Peter to put out into deep water and let down the nets for a catch.

This is the point at which Peter shone. He did what Jesus asked him to do. He could have found all kinds of reasons for refusing. Night was the time to fish and they had tried all night without success. Now it was morning and they were tired and discouraged. It was time to rest for another try the next night. But Peter didn't use all those excuses that he could have come up with for not doing what Jesus asked. Having failed, he was willing to try again. We see here what we might call Peter's higher self. Hopefully, in him, we can discover the higher self that is within us.

The Counterpoint

Then, right on the heels of this trustful action, this venturing out into the deep water, there comes the counterpoint, the contradiction. Right after we see a glimpse of Peter's higher self, we see very clearly his lower self. Peter fell on his knees and said, "Depart from me, for I am a sinful man, O Lord."

Peter had had so much success that we would think that he would have thought well of himself, but here we see the opposite. His feeling of guilt and failure and self-disgust took over. Here was a time when he could have relished this moment of being with Jesus and been happy for the successful catch, but Peter was so caught up in his feelings of sinfulness that he couldn't enjoy it. He listened to the voice of his lower self and asked Jesus to depart from him.

So often, people see us one way and we see ourselves so much differently. Søren Kierkegaard, the Danish philosopher and theologian, confessed this when he said, "I have just now come from a party where I was its life and soul; witticisms streamed from my lips, everyone laughed and admired me, but I went away . . . and wanted to shoot myself."

It was that kind of feeling that engulfed Peter. One of the reasons it is good to look to him as an example, a pattern of what it means to be a Christian, is that his bad side shows as clearly as his good. His lower self is as clear as his higher self. He makes no effort to hide it. This can give us perspective and the courage to deal with this side in ourselves.

Counter Counterpoint

A famous opera singer was asked the secret of his power and authority in singing. He answered: "A long time ago I was given understanding by a master teacher that there is a little me and a big me within me. The little me is fearful, superstitious, and weak; when I go on stage I repeat over and over again, 'Big me, come forth from within and sing.' The big me has never let me down."

I know that like Peter and the opera singer, I, too, have a big me and a little me. I guess I like Peter better than the opera singer because his big me sometimes let him down. That makes me more comfortable. Yet, what the opera singer is sharing has great meaning. In each event that we are facing, in each issue of life, we can recognize the big me and the little me. We are going to have to decide which one we are going to listen to, which one we are going to let come forth. We need to listen and appeal to the larger me that is within us.

If we are just looking at ourselves, we can easily get caught up in a kind of narcissism. This is a part of our age and has a lot of appeal. Just think of all the books that are selling which foster this kind of self-oriented attitude.

Jesus suggested just the opposite, namely self-forgetfulness, to Peter as the way to rise above the contradictions within himself. He said, "Do not be afraid—from now on you will be catching men." He gave him a mission that reached out beyond himself. As he reached out to others in fulfillment of that mission, he was able to develop the higher self within him. In seeking to be faithful to Jesus' command to love others, he could even grow to love himself. In helping others to find their higher self, he found his.

Others can't move us to choose this higher self. It is something that we must do ourselves. Neither can we do it alone. We can't do it unless we open ourselves to the love of Christ and the love of each other. This is the nourishment we need to feed us on this journey to become what we can be. The church should be the place where we seek to grow as persons ourselves and seek to give others the acceptance and support that will create the climate of security that will allow such growth to take place in them. That is what it means for us to be fishers of persons.

Caught up in our own feelings of sinfulness, guilt, failure, we need to hear and respond to the challenge our Lord gave to Peter: "Follow me—and do not be afraid."

If we wish to move beyond the turmoil between the point and counterpoint within us, between our higher and lower self, we need to accept the mission that Christ gives us.

Matthew 16:13–26

Now when Jesus came into the district of Caesarea Philippi, he asked his disciples, "Who do men say that the Son of man is?" And they said, "Some say John the Baptist, others say Elijah, and others Jeremiah or one of the prophets." He said to them, "But who do you say that I am?" Simon Peter replied, "You are the Christ, the Son of the living God." And Jesus answered him, "Blessed are you, Simon Bar-Jona! For flesh and blood has not revealed this to you, but my Father who is in heaven. And I tell you, you are Peter, and on this rock I will build my church, and the powers of death shall not prevail against it. I will give you the keys of the kingdom of heaven, and whatever you bind on earth shall be bound in heaven, and whatever you loose on earth shall be loosed in heaven." Then he strictly charged the disciples to tell no one that he was the Christ.

From that time Jesus began to show his disciples that he must go to Jerusalem and suffer many things from the elders and chief priests and scribes, and be killed, and on the third day be raised. And Peter took him and began to rebuke him, saying, "God forbid, Lord! This shall never happen to you." But he turned and said to Peter, "Get behind me, Satan! You are a hindrance to me; for you are not on the side of God, but of men."

Then Jesus told his disciples, "If any man would come after me, let him deny himself and take up his cross and follow me. For whoever would save his life will lose it, and whoever loses his life for my sake will find it. For what will it profit a man, if he gains the whole world and forfeits his life? Or what shall a man give in return for his life?

3

Twice As Many Ears

Affirmation

"And Jesus answered him, 'Blessed are you Simon Bar-Jona! For flesh and blood has not revealed this to you, but my Father who is in heaven. And I tell you, you are Peter, and on this rock I will build my church, and the powers of death shall not prevail against it.'"

This is the text upon which the Roman Catholic church bases its position in regard to the pope and the church. It is also extremely significant because of Peter's recognition of Jesus as the Messiah. Rather than approach this account in traditional ways, let us focus on the relationship of Peter and Jesus.

When that is our approach, we see dynamics to the story that may have escaped us previously. To the forefront comes the realization that Jesus' words to Peter were a tremendous compliment. We also need to realize how extremely important Jesus' words of praise and accommodation were to Peter and to their relationship, since those words preceeded some negative and even condemning comments.

How much easier it is for us to accept negative comments or criticism from someone who has also expressed appreciation for other things we have said or done. It is much more difficult to field negative comments from people who will tell you your faults, but won't take the time or the effort to say something positive.

What we need, then, is gratitude for each other. We need the sensitivity and the honesty to look for the good in each other, rather than just react to what we think is bad. This is part of what it means to follow Jesus as Master, for surely it is the path along which he leads us, if we will but follow.

One man was having trouble with his appliances. He called up three days in a row and did not get any satisfaction. His blood pressure mounted with his anger. Finally, the company sent a repairman who looked as if he had been dragged through Mary Poppins's chimney. By then the customer was not only angry but also disappointed because he wondered how this grimy mechanic could do anything effectively.

Despite his anger and disappointment, the customer said to himself, "I am a Christian. I will control myself." He then approached the serviceman saying, "I am sure you have had a hard day and you wish you weren't here. You probably don't find any glamor in repairing these old machines that will only break down again, but I am most appreciative that you have come to help me."

The repairman looked at him and said, "Say that again, please." The repairman on his own initiative came back the next day with brand new parts and said, "These are better and I am going to replace the ones I put in for temporary repair. I want to do a good job for you."

So often, we rob ourselves and others of joy and satisfaction with our grumbling and complaining. If the time comes when negatives need to be shared for honesty to survive in a relationship, how much better will be the result if we first take the time to appreciate the other person.

Confrontation

"And Peter took him and began to rebuke him saying, 'God forbid, Lord! This shall never happen to you.' But *Jesus* turned and said to Peter, 'Get behind me, Satan. You are a hindrance (a stumblingblock) to me; for you are not on the side of God, but of men.'"

We could try to justify these words of Jesus by launching into a discussion of how important it is to be open and honest with each other. I've done that before, too, and I think I have missed something. I've missed really looking at the feelings of Peter and Jesus. Put yourself for a moment in Peter's shoes. The man you have left your home to follow, whom you have just recognized as the Messiah, has told you that he will suffer and die. You love him. You don't want to see him suffer, let alone die. So you try to express that love you have by saying, "Heaven forbid that that will happen." Then the one you love looks at you and says, "Away with you." He calls you "Satan" and tells you that you are a hindrance, a stumblingblock to him. Can you feel with Peter? Can you feel the bite of those words? Can you sense how they must have hurt?

How easy it would have been for Peter then to express his anger toward Jesus, perhaps to tell him off. How easy it would have been to react to the hurt that he felt and mouth off rather than to step back from the situation and try to understand why Jesus had responded to him in the angry way he did.

The ancient Greek philosopher Zeno said, "We have two ears, but only one mouth, that we might hear more and speak less." Perhaps, that is God's way in creation of telling us that we should do twice as much listening as we do mouthing off. We are to listen not merely to the words of the other person, but be attentive to their feelings. Our face, our eyes, the set of our jaw, the way we carry ourselves, all indicate to the person that will take note how the other is feeling. Maybe that is also why we have twice as many eyes.

I have the feeling that Peter loved Jesus enough that he paid attention to his feelings and not just his words. Why do you imagine that Jesus was so uptight in regard to what Peter said? Peter was really only expressing his love and his wish that Jesus would not suffer. Peter had hit a sensitive nerve. He had touched the point at which Jesus was facing great personal struggle. Jesus didn't want to suffer. He had no desire to die. He was struggling with giving up his own self and his own desires in order that he might do what God wished. He was fully human, therefore, it wasn't easy.

Let your mind go back to the temptation experience that Jesus faced at the beginning of his ministry. In Luke, we find that account ending with this statement: "And when the devil had ended every temptation, he departed from him until an opportune time." Well, this was the time. It was his dear friend Peter, his disciple, that under the mantle of love, confronted him with the same temptation Satan had tried in the wilderness. Now, we can begin to see why Jesus called Peter, "Satan." Peter was confronting Jesus with the temptation to escape the cross. William Barclay says, "That is why Peter was Satan. Satan literally means the Adversary. That is why Peter's ideas were not God's but men's. Satan is any force which seeks to deflect us from the way of God: Satan is any influence which seeks to make us turn back from the hard way that God has set before us; Satan is any power who seeks to make human desires take the place of the divine imperative" (William Barclay, *The Daily Bible Study Series;* The Gospel of Matthew, Vol. 2 [Philadelphia: Westminster Press, 1957], p.164).

Reconciliation

"Jesus then said to his disciples, 'If anyone wishes to be a follower of mine, he must leave self behind; he must take up his cross and come with me. Whoever cares for his own safety is lost; but if a man will let himself be lost for my sake, he will find his true self' " (NEB).

Here we are moved from Jesus' own personal struggle with self to his telling the disciples that they must also see that struggle through if they are to find their true selves. We also must go through the same struggle if we are to be the Lord's disciples. Discipleship is not a matter of simply believing things about Jesus and that he died on the cross for our sins. If, indeed, we are to claim that we are Christians, it means that we must be willing to bear the cross in our own lives. This means leaving self behind in order that our true self might be found. Bearing the cross of Jesus means that we subject our willful selves to God's will for us.

Peter had to struggle to leave self behind. There was a time when he avoided the cross, when he said he didn't know Christ and wasn't even one of his followers.

We know what Peter did in leading the disciples and founding the church. It brings us up short to realize that all of that could have been spoiled by this interchange of words described in the scripture passage. Peter must have had empathy for Christ. Empathy means being able to share in another person's emotions in such a way that we might speak and act with compassion. Peter didn't respond angrily to Jesus, because he didn't think merely about how Jesus' words hurt him. He left self behind enough so that he could realize that for Jesus to say what he did in the way that he did, he must have been troubled in some way. Peter was able to think of the reasons behind Jesus' words, and this may have saved their relationship from being destroyed.

A young teacher had the honesty to describe in a very personal way her relationship with a particular pupil. She said, "Jamie, a pupil in my second grade, taught me a lesson that will affect my relationship with others as long as I live. It was one of those days common to first-year teachers. Even my most angelic pupils' halos were decidedly askew—and if Jamie ever had a halo, I had failed to notice it."

"Jamie was my most trying pupil. What had seemed innocent mischief at the first of the year was fast approaching malicious destruction—this in spite of my constant reprimands. That day in particular he was at his worst. He deliberately knocked a potted plant from the window sill. He ripped a picture from the hall bulletin board. Then, just as the dismissal bell rang, he slammed a locker door on Randy's finger. Randy howled with pain.

"That was the last straw. I grabbed Jamie and shook him hard. 'You've done one bad thing after another all day long, Jamie!' I stormed. 'You are a bad boy!' Jamie was used to my scolding, but never before had he seen me so angry. For a moment he stared at me, his blue eyes wide with shocked surprise. Then, his defiant little body crumpled and the tears welled up. He pulled away and scrubbed his eyes with the back of his grubby hand.

" 'I know I'm bad—most of the time I'm bad,' he said. For a moment he was silent, fighting the tears. Then, he added, 'Sometimes I try to do good things—only then, nobody ever notices.'

"Slowly he followed the others out the door. No one waited for him. He had no friends. Badly shaken, I returned to my desk and asked myself for the thousandth time what I was doing wrong—why I was failing with Jamie.

"And then suddenly the thought struck me that I never tried to understand Jamie from the point of view of his needs, his need for attention and love. Rather, I always considered him from my need for discipline in the classroom."

We make that same mistake, don't we, with our children, our mate, as well as other people? The lesson that young teacher learned about looking at other people from the point of their needs and not just our own is a lesson we desperately need to apply in our daily living. I believe that that is at the heart of what Jesus meant when he said that we must leave self behind in order to find our true selves.

Mark 14:53–54, 66–72

And they led Jesus to the high priest; and all the chief priests and the elders and the scribes were assembled. And Peter had followed him at a distance, right into the courtyard of the high priest; and he was sitting with the guards, and warming himself at the fire.

And as Peter was below in the courtyard, one of the maids of the high priest came; and seeing Peter warming himself, she looked at him, and said, "You also were with the Nazarene, Jesus." But he denied it, saying, "I neither know nor understand what you mean." And he went out into the gateway. And the maid saw him, and began again to say to the bystanders, "This man is one of them." But again he denied it. And after a little while again the bystanders said to Peter, "Certainly you are one of them; for you are a Galilean." But he began to invoke a curse on himself and to swear, "I do not know this man of whom you speak." And immediately the cock crowed a second time. And Peter remembered how Jesus had said to him, "Before the cock crows twice, you will deny me three times." And he broke down and wept.

4

Construction Kits

Someone has said that there are three classes of people: those who watch things happen, those who don't know what is happening, and those who make things happen. I suppose that we are tempted to put people in those kinds of categories. The beauty of the story of Peter is that we see in one person all three classes of people. They are stages of life that he experienced. Hopefully, as we look at Peter, we can summon the courage to face where we are and to move on to where we should be.

When We Watch Things Happen

"And Peter followed him at a distance, right into the courtyard of the high priest's; and he was sitting with the guards, warming himself at the fire."

We have spoken of this scene so often in terms of Peter's denial that our familiarity has robbed us of its deepest meanings. It is true that Peter denied that he knew Christ three times. This was not a mistake of one who lacked courage, for he had just showed reckless courage when he drew his sword in the Garden of Gethsemane. It was not the mistake of one who lacked faith in Jesus. It was Peter alone who had the faith after having run away with the others when they seized Jesus, to head back, following him at a distance right into the courtyard of the high priest's house. When he was recognized as one who had been with Jesus, true, he denied it. The temptation would have been to clear out then and there while the getting was good. But he stayed. That took faith. It happened again and he stayed. That took faith. It happened a third time. It took faith to stay there.

Well, if Peter showed courage, if Peter showed faith, what, then, was his mistake? Peter's mistake was that he confused what he believed about Jesus with true discipleship. He was in that courtyard waiting for Jesus to show everyone that he was the Son of God. He was waiting for Jesus to do something that would set him free, change the situation, and it didn't happen. What Peter expected to happen never came about.

Sometimes when we make a mistake, we fault other people. In today's terms, that is giving someone else your monkey. When we have a problem and we toss it to somebody else to solve, that is giving someone else your monkey. Mature persons accept responsibility for their own behavior. Mature persons keep their own monkey instead of trying to pass it off on somebody else.

You know, sometimes we have tried to pass off as faith what is really monkey business. I have had people say that they have a particular problem and then go on to state, "I'm not going to worry about it any more because I have given it to Jesus. If I need to stop what I'm doing, he will find a way to stop me." That is monkey business. It sounds a lot better than it is. It sounds like you have a lot of faith. There is a great deal of talk about Jesus and belief. When you discard all the God language, it is putting your monkey on Jesus. That is being irresponsible.

This is where Peter appears to be at this stage of his spiritual journey. He seemed to all the epitome of faith, but it was the faith of one who wanted to watch things happen. He said that he didn't know Jesus. Maybe he was telling the truth, for he was still too filled with *his* ideas of what Jesus should be.

When We Don't Know What Is Happening

"He began to invoke a curse on himself and to swear, 'I do not know this man of whom you speak.' And immediately a cock crowed. And Peter remembered how Jesus had said to him, 'Before the cock crows twice, you will deny me three times.' "

Peter had reached his breaking point. He just didn't know what was happening to Jesus, nor to himself. He didn't know quite what to do. Peter was alone and away from Jesus. This often is what happens when we are separated from Jesus, whether we are willing to see our situation in those terms or not.

Crises in our lives are usually painful, particularly when there is an inner struggle, a trying to come to grips with ourselves. Yet, as painful as those times are, they cause us to break out of our old patterns of behavior. We need that stimulus to force us to find new ways of dealing with others and ourselves. This was also true of Peter. His time of confusion, of discord without and within, was needed to move him beyond the narrow faith he had in Jesus and himself.

One is not hard pressed to give examples of people who simply don't know what is happening. I was trying to interest a man in coming back to church some time ago. He assured me that he didn't have anything against me or this church. But he blamed my church for having appointed a Black pastor as my predecessor to this congregation. After hearing about that at length and trying to explain how our system works and some of the factors in that situation, I could see I wasn't getting anywhere. So I said, "Well, this is my ninth year of appointment here. That is long past and a lot of new and exciting things are happening now." Well, he had something else that was making him angry. He thought that we shouldn't send any money for missions outside the United States. We should look after our own. He made a passionate plea for helping causes like those in Appalachia. I asked him if he knew what missionary family we supported. He didn't have any idea that his own church was supporting a family in Kentucky. I asked if he knew about our young people going last summer for a work project to the Red Bird Mission in Kentucky. He didn't. "Well," I said, "we are doing what you seem to believe we should and we could use your interest and support." It didn't make any difference in his attitude.

Some people don't know what is happening and we usually pass it off as lacking information. If that were so, upon receiving the information, we would change. More often than we would like to admit, we don't know what is happening inside ourselves and we aren't willing to struggle enough to find out. Without Jesus, I don't know that we have the courage to face ourselves. I think that the reverse is true as well. If we haven't had the courage to face ourselves, I don't think we really know Jesus however much we talk about him. Without both, we really don't know what is happening in life.

When We Make Things Happen

"And he flung his cloak about his head and wept."

Peter was ashamed. How symbolic it is that he covered his face. That is what we usually do when we are ashamed, isn't it? We try to hide our mistakes, our failures, our sin. What it all adds up to is that we don't know each other, or ourselves, because we are trying so hard to seem different than we really are.

A minister, walking down a street, saw a crowd of boys with a dog. He walked over to them and asked them what they were doing. One boy responded. "We are having a contest to see who can tell the biggest lie. The one who tells the biggest gets the dog as a prize." The minister responded, "Why, that's terrible! You know, it is wrong to tell a lie. When I was a boy, I never told a lie!" One little fellow turned to the minister and said, "Here, mister, you win our puppy dog!"   That is a fun story, but there is more than just humor in it. We try so hard to put on such a front. I don't think that we are as convincing to others as we would like to think. It takes a coming to grips with ourselves to remove the cloak and let others see our tears.

Have you ever wondered how we learned about this story? It seems feasible that Peter told the story about himself. When he did, he moved from being someone who didn't know what was happening to one who made things happen. He became the one who preached at Pentecost, who led the early church, who made things happen. If we are going to make that same spiritual journey, we must travel the same road.

The other day, I invited a woman to become a member of our church. She had been coming regularly, so I thought the chances were good that she would respond favorably to the invitation. To my surprise, she broke down and cried. She said that she wasn't worthy to be a member of the church. She felt too bad about herself to belong. I responded by telling her that we are all sinners and that we don't join the fellowship of the church because we have reached some level of goodness in our life. We join because we know that we need God's help and the help of one another even to begin to be what God wants us to be. I spoke of God's grace, God's love as a gift that we don't earn or ever merit. Unfortunately, she is still too caught up in those feelings about herself to accept that.

So often, we as the church spend enormous energy maintaining an image of being good and respectable people. Yet, there is a big difference between our outer self that we let others see and our inner self that we don't reveal. We need to take down the cloak from about our head so that all persons will know that they are where they belong, so that we can know each other and ourselves.

The truth is that we are not completed products. We are more like construction kits that aren't fully assembled. God has given us all the parts that we need to make a life that is worthwhile. We have the instructions on how to put the pieces together. We have each other to help out. Yet, it is up to us to put it together. It is not God's way to do things for us, but to encourage and enable us to do things for ourselves.

How much of our construction kit we finally put together will depend on whether we want puppy dogs or eternal life. Who will we pattern ourselves after? Will we be dishonest about ourselves and pretend to be all put together or shall we be open with one another?

If it is eternal life that we seek, and we wish to find ourselves as did Peter, we need to experience the presence of the risen Christ in our life, not as the One who will assume our responsibilities, but as the One who will help us be a responsible person. That is how we can move from being a person who watches things happen, or doesn't know what is happening, to one who makes things happen.

John 8:31–32

Jesus then said to the Jews who had believed in him, "If you continue in my word, you are truly my disciples, and you will know the truth, and the truth will make you free."

5

Shedding Skins

At a funeral service recently, actually at the grave, I had a strange intuition that one of the young ladies there, a member of the grieving family, was experiencing something more than the death of her grandmother. I walked over to her and said, "I have the feeling that you are about ready to shed a skin." She immediately launched into telling me about what she had experienced just the night before and the emotional bombardment that she felt.

I knew nothing about what she revealed before she shared it. I know why I felt intuitively what she was going through, though I did not know any of the details. I knew, because in recent months I have been going through the process of shedding a skin, perhaps a number of them, myself. I don't know quite how to say it, but when you are in the full throes of such an experience, you can sense who else is going through the same process.

Because of what I am going through as a person, I have gone back and read biblical accounts which simply jump off the page with meaning I had never discovered before, no matter how many times I had read them. We will continue to look at the apostle Peter to discover how his relationship with Jesus brought about growth in him as a person. Growth has been defined by one physician as "a common process available to all men who are offered circumstances which arouse an awareness of themselves and a trustworthy, lasting, and honest relationship with someone who can stand to be loved, hated, rejected, and depended upon while he assists in the birth of new life" (Dr. George Benson, M.D., "Death and Dying: A Psychoanalytic Perspective"; The Journal of Pastoral Care, June 1972). That is exactly what Jesus offered to Peter and exactly what Jesus offers us.

Finding the Center of Your Life

Our Lord said, "If you make my message the fixed center of your life, you really are my disciples."

It has been said that to be strong at the circumference a person must be strong at the center. Perhaps, our ultimate task might be seen as finding the real center of our life. Most of us are running around doing so many things that we never really get at that. We don't get at it, not because we don't realize that it should be done or because we don't see it as important, but because we are all basically afraid to meet ourselves and deal with ourselves. I like Peter because that struggle within him is so vivid.

In the fifth chapter of Luke, we are told the story of how Jesus got into Simon Peter's boat and asked him to push out a little way from the land. Jesus sat down in the boat and taught the crowd from there. After he had finished speaking, he turned to Simon and asked him to push out into deep water and to let down his nets for a catch. Simon responded by saying that they had worked hard all night and had caught nothing. Nonetheless, he did as the Lord asked, and they caught so many fish that the nets were filled to the breaking point.

Simon accepted the authority of Christ and did as he asked. He could very well have wondered just what the carpenter had to say to the fisherman about fishing. Simon did as Jesus asked and the catch was plentiful. Simon's response to the catch was odd. He threw himself at the feet of Jesus and said, "Leave me, for I am a sinful man." Jesus replied to Simon, "From now on, it will be men that you catch." That whole exchange sounds strange until you really look at it carefully enough to uncover its power.

Peter brought up the matter of his sinfulness. Jesus did not respond by speaking to his sins. He spoke to his fears. The reason why Jesus did not speak to Peter's sins was because Peter's talk about them was a defense, a comfortable distraction away from the truth which Peter feared. It may be that the Lord is far less interested in our sins than we presume. So much of our energy is spent on dealing out punishment to ourselves for our past mistakes or worrying about potential future problems. The Lord calls us to give up our self-centered preoccupations so that we can live the present to the fullest and not fritter away our energy. So when Peter brought up the matter of his sinfulness Jesus didn't even deal with either sin or forgiveness. Instead, Jesus said that his life task was to catch persons rather than merely catch fish. It boiled down to the challenge to put Christ's message at the center of his life and truly to become his disciple. Christ puts that challenge before us, too.

Facing the Truth About Ourselves

"If you continue in my word, you are truly my disciples, and you will know the truth . . . "

We like to think that this "truth" involves certain theological or biblical affirmations, or an assortment of emotional experiences. We try to make it only that because, like Peter, we are afraid to deal with the truth about ourselves. So the truth is kept as something external, or watered down so as to allow ourselves to be fooled into thinking that we have really let Christ change our lives. It may be closer to the truth to say that our language has changed but not our lives.

Even though Peter was the first to proclaim Jesus as the Messiah, even though Peter belonged to the inner circle of the disciples and shared the momentous experiences with Christ that we read about in the Bible, he still had a hard time dealing with himself. It was very difficult for him to throw off his old self and become the new person Christ wanted him to be.

Think of that scene where Jesus was trying to get the disciples to face the reality of his crucifixion. Jesus said to them: "There is not one of you whose courage will stand the test, for scripture says: 'I will smite the shepherd and the sheep will be scattered. But after I have risen, I will go on ahead of you into Galilee.' Peter said to him: 'Even if everyone else's courage fails, mine will not.' "

Jesus' talk about his suffering brought about the fear and psychological regression that we see in the childish bravado of Peter. Like a brave boy following his hero, Peter made his way to Pilate's courtyard. It was there he denied Jesus. It was there that he was forced to come face to face with the truth about himself. It was not only the time for Christ to die, but the time as well for the death of the old Peter. It was the time for the death of the naïve, immature Peter. The time had come when Peter could no longer avoid coming to grips with himself.

What a beautiful job he had done to set himself up for self-punishment! "Even if everyone else's courage fails, mine will not." "If I have to die with you, I will never disown you." Peter was human: his courage failed and he avoided dying with Christ. I imagine that he let those statements torment him. I imagine that he was wracked with guilt. A process of disintegration must have taken place in Peter's life, where the pieces of himself seemed to be splitting apart and where he was forced to deal with feelings about himself that he had never dared to face, but which he could now no longer avoid. We see glimpses of this in the gospel account.

That process involves more than merely facing certain facts about oneself. It leads to mourning. We experience a sense of loss that must be grieved even though we are getting rid of an immature part of ourselves. That is what Peter had to do. He mourned not only Jesus' death, but also the loss of that part of himself which had been brought about by Jesus' death.

Feeling the Freedom That Comes When One Finally Meets Self

" . . . you will know the truth and the truth will set you free."

Gail Sheehy, in her book, *Passages*, speaks of the decade between 35 and 45 as one of both danger and opportunity. We may feel the need as never before to rework the narrow identity by which we defined ourselves in the first half of life. Those that respond to that challenge may find that they have entered a full authenticity crisis. There may come the realization that if you don't use this time to change what you don't like about yourself, you never will. There is a tremendous sense of urgency and vulnerability.

She says, "It is frightening to step off onto the treacherous footbridge leading to the second half of life. We can't take everything with us on this journey through uncertainty. Along the way, we discover that we are alone. There is grieving to be done because an old self is dying. By taking in our suppressed and even our unwanted parts, we prepare at the gut level for the reintegration of an identity that is ours and ours alone—not some artificial form put together to please the culture or our mates. It is a dark passage at the beginning. But by disassembling ourselves, we can glimpse the light and gather our parts into a renewal" (*Passages* [New York: E. P. Dutton & Co., 1974), p. 30.

I don't believe that I am merely projecting my own experience upon Peter when I say that this is what he went through following the death of Christ. Let us try to see how Peter coped with loss and grief. It was at Pentecost. At Pentecost we see the result of an accomplished mourning process, not only for Christ, but also for the death of Peter's old self.

It was Peter's sermon that led the way for 3,000 to accept Christ. It was not because he worked especially hard on that sermon, but because there was a new Peter. When we have the courage to face and give up immature and unwanted aspects of ourselves, there comes a bursting release of new energy. That new energy emerges upon you as joy. Even the simplest things of life have new meaning: food—new taste, friendship—new meaning, marriage—a new sense of adventure. You can find the opposite of what we call loneliness.

I like the story about Harry Truman in his retirement in Independence, Missouri. He enjoyed answering the questions of groups of school children who visited him at the Truman Library. Merle Miller in his biography of Harry Truman reports that "on one day I like to remember, the last question came from an anxious, small boy with red hair whose ears had grown up, but not his face. 'Mr. President,' he said, as if his future and the world's depended on the reply, 'Was you popular when you was a boy?' The President looked at the boy over the glasses that always made him look like an irritated owl. 'Why, no,' he said, 'I was never popular. The popular boys were the ones who were good at games and had big tight fists. I was never like that. Without my glasses I was blind as a bat, and to tell the truth, I was kind of a sissy. If there was any danger of getting into a fight, I always ran. I guess that's why I'm here today.' The little boy started to applaud, and then everybody else did, too. It was an eminently satisfactory answer for all of us who ever ran from a fight, which is all of us." (Merle Miller, *Plain Speaking: An Oral Biography of Harry S. Truman*[New York: Berkley Publishing Corp., 1973], pp. 34–35.) This could only have been said by someone who may have run from fights as a boy, but who finally, somewhere along the line, had stopped running from himself.

The truth will make you free.

Luke 22:31–34

"Simon, Simon, behold, Satan demanded to have you, that he might sift you like wheat, but I have prayed for you that your faith may not fail; and when you have turned again, strengthen your brethren." And he said to him, "Lord, I am ready to go with you to prison and to death." He said, "I tell you, Peter, the cock will not crow this day, until you three times deny that you know me."

6

The Resurrection of Peter

It seems that one of the mistakes that we have made as Christians is to have associated Easter too thoroughly with the life God has promised after this earthly life is through. That certainty is comforting to us, particularly as it strengthens us at the time of the death of a loved one. We have such a tremendous denial of our own mortality, though, that somehow the Easter hope gets projected far off into a vague future. The result is that the real impact that it could have on our lives in the present is lost for the most part. The good news that needs to be conveyed is that Easter has to do with the here and now. We need to see Friday of Holy Week as it intersects with the suffering we are going through. We need to see Saturday of Holy Week as the time between the suffering we know too well and the victory we haven't yet experienced. We need to see Easter not merely as some far-off event having to do with heaven, but more as the time when God lifts us up and we see a new day dawning for our life. Phillips Brooks put it this way: "The great Easter truth is not that we are to live newly after death, but that we are to be new here and now by the power of the resurrection."

In our pursuit to learn more about Peter, let us consider his resurrection. We can identify with Peter's struggles. He has an eager love for Jesus Christ and yet he stumbles and falls as he seeks to live out his discipleship. As we see his struggle unfold, we can see the road that we must travel.

The Sifting

"Simon, Simon, behold, Satan demanded to have you, that he might sift you like wheat . . . "

Jesus was a genius in conveying the eternal truths of God in terms of the daily experience of the people to whom he spoke. Visualize the scene with me that Jesus had in mind. The wheat had matured in the fields. It had been cut by a sickle and had been laid to dry on the hard threshing floor, out in the open under the warm sun. The wheat kernels had been separated from the straw. Men with large shovels would throw it into the air over and over again. The wheat would fall to the ground, but the chaff would go flying in the air where the wind would take it. Often this was done at night when the wind was the strongest. One could see clouds of chaff in the air. It would get in your eyes, on your clothes, in your hair.

Jesus knew that it was the last night of his earthly life that he would spend with his disciples. Indeed, the time of harvest had come. It was nighttime, the time when the sifting was to take place. The chaff had to be removed. As long as it is with the wheat, the wheat is bitter and hard. The wheat is not good until the chaff has been purged. Until the time of sifting, you really can't see the chaff. So it was for Peter. After Jesus said that he would be sifted like wheat, he replied back confidently, "Lord, I am ready to go with you to prison and death." Jesus knew Peter better than Peter knew himself and replied, "I tell you, Peter, the cock will not crow tonight until you have three times over denied that you know me."

As Peter sat there that night, he seemed to represent those who were most committed to Jesus. After all, it had been three years before that he left everything behind to follow him. He was the first to declare that Jesus was the Messiah. He was not only one of the twelve disciples, but one of the three with whom Jesus shared his most momentous experiences. He knew Jesus, but he didn't know himself.

So it is with us. We are so astute at hiding our problems, our struggles, our sins from each other, that we often don't know ourselves. It is as we open up to each other in an honest way that we find out who we are and what we are like. We like to hone in on the mistakes of others and be really honest about how we feel about them, but we are so dishonest about ourselves.

Now is the time for the sifting to take place. Maybe others can't see the chaff in your life as long as it is with the wheat. Whether we like it or not, they can taste the bitterness. When we start to deal honestly with our life, all that chaff is going to be seen. It will seem to get on everything when the sifting is going on. Only as we are sifted can we be made into the bread of life.

An Unfailing Friend

"Simon, Simon, behold, Satan demanded to have you, that he might sift you like wheat; but I have prayed for you that your faith may not fail . . ."

That very night Peter indeed denied knowing Christ three times. I think that he must have been tempted to do what we so often do, namely, to rationalize his mistakes. He could have said to himself, "What else could I do with all those soldiers around?" He could have compared himself favorably to others saying to himself, "The others didn't even follow Christ that far. It was because I cared so much that I got myself into that predicament."

What made the difference do you think? Do you think that Peter was made out of better stuff than we are? I don't think so. Do you think that he was that much more committed to Christ than we are? Perhaps not. What made the difference then? I think that he remembered that Jesus, having said that he would be sifted, went on to say, "but for you I have prayed that your faith may not fail . . ."

That will also mark the difference whether we will go on rationalizing our mistakes, our sins, or whether we can face up to them. Do you know in your heart that Jesus is praying for you that your faith may not fail? Do you know that? If you do, then you know what Peter needed to know, that despite all his mistakes, Jesus loved him. You can't earn his love, you can't earn anybody's love. It is a gift. You have but to receive it and love in return.

What a beautiful moment it is in the Easter story when Jesus made a special point that Peter should be told about the resurrection. Do you see the implications of that concern? Jesus wanted Peter to know that he still accepted him, that he was his friend even though his faith had faltered. That is the kind of friend that we have in Jesus.

A few years before his death, it is reported that the giant of theologians, Karl Barth, was asked the following question by an American interviewer: "Dr. Barth, you have probably written more words than any other person in the history of Christianity about what the gospel of Jesus Christ really means. If you were to sum up in one sentence all of your thinking about what the good news of Jesus Christ means to you, what would you say?" According to the story, Professor Barth sat back in his chair, puffed thoughtfully on his pipe for a moment, and then with a twinkle in his eye, came forth with this response: "Jesus loves me, this I know, for the Bible tells me so."

That's it! That is the good news! It is for you! Jesus loves you. As he said to Peter, so he is saying to us, "But I have prayed for you that your faith may not fail." I came across a definition of faith the other day that really speaks to me. "Faith is facing the unknown future and the uncharted journey with an unfailing friend." What a friend we have in Jesus!!!

The Call to Serve

"Simon, Simon, behold, Satan demanded to have you, that he might sift you like wheat; but I have prayed for you that your faith may not fail; and when you have turned again, strengthen your brethren."

There are three parts to that message of Jesus to Peter. Our temptation is to get stuck in the second section. We need to know that Jesus is praying for us. We need to know that Jesus loves us. We need to know that as we face the unknown future and the uncharted journey that we won't walk alone. However, just as Jesus moved Peter's focus away from himself, so we need to let our Lord help us to do that very thing. " . . . when you have come to yourself, you must lend strength to your brothers" (NEB).

Have you ever thought how terribly selfish and self-centered some of the hymns are that we love to sing the most? "Blessed assurance, Jesus is mine. Perfect submission, all is at rest; I in my Savior am happy and blest, watching and waiting, looking above, filled with his goodness, lost in his love." Lost in ourselves would be more like it. "Rock of Ages, cleft for me, let me hide myself in thee . . . " Great tunes and terrible theology.

Called to be sanctified, we too often end up being only sanctimonius. Called to be set apart for sacred duty, too often we end up with hypocritical devoutness. We sing, "Hide me, O my Savior hide, till the storm of life is past" as if that is what being a follower of Jesus Christ is all about. That goes against everything Jesus said and stood for. "For whoever would save his life will lose it; and whoever loses his life for my sake and the gospel's will save it."

In so many of these hymns that we like to sing, have you noticed the absence of real concern, of real love for other people? In so many of these hymns that we like to sing, have you noticed the absence of a real involvement in life, in the lives of others? If you haven't, have you also been unwilling to see it in yourself?

Hal Luccock tells of the man who bought a couple of new suits for himself, and then purchased a nineteen-cent handkerchief for his wife and drove home singing, "I love my Nancy Jane." It was pretty obvious whom he really loved, no matter what he was singing. Maybe he didn't see it, but others could. Regardless of all we sing about loving Christ, how we act toward others will show just whom we love.

Peter could have become stuck in the second section. He certainly had tremendous feelings of guilt and remorse. How easy it would have been for him to focus on the love Jesus had for him and play that theme over and over again, seeking to answer the cries of guilt that sprang from deep within his soul. Peter not only remembered Jesus saying, "but for you I have prayed that your faith may not fail . . . ", but he also remembered Jesus having said, "and when you have come to yourself, you must lend strength to your brothers." That is what we need to hear the Lord saying to us. We need to let him show us how to get beyond ourselves, so that we too can accept our calling to lend strength to each other.

There is a beautiful story in Exodus about Moses receiving

strength when weary in battle. As long as Moses held up his hands, he and his men won against the Amalekites. He grew so tired, though, that he could no longer hold up his hands. So "Aaron and Hur held up his hands, one on one side, and the other on the other side; so his hands were steady until the going down of the sun" (Exodus 17:12).

There have been times in my life when my arms were tired and I couldn't hold them up by myself any longer. Praise God, there were those who came and held them up for me. Being the church to one another means that we help hold up each other's arms when we are weak.

It is only when we respond to Jesus' summons to lend strength to our neighbor that we can experience the power of resurrection.

John 21:1–19

After this Jesus revealed himself again to the disciples by the Sea of Tiberias; and he revealed himself in this way. Simon Peter, Thomas called the Twin, Nathanael of Cana in Galilee, the sons of Zeb'edee, and two others of his disciples were together. Simon Peter said to them, "I am going fishing." They said to him, "We will go with you." They went out and got into the boat; but that night they caught nothing.

Just as day was breaking, Jesus stood on the beach; yet the disciples did not know that it was Jesus. Jesus said to them, "Children, have you any fish?" They answered him, "No." He said to them, "Cast the net on the right side of the boat, and you will find some." So they cast it, and now they were not able to haul it in, for the quantity of fish. That disciple whom Jesus loved said to Peter, "It is the Lord!" When Simon Peter heard that it was the Lord, he put on his clothes, for he was stripped for work, and sprang into the sea. But the other disciples came in the boat, dragging the net full of fish, for they were not far from the land, but about a hundred yards off.

When they got out on land, they saw a charcoal fire there, with fish lying on it, and bread. Jesus said to them, "Bring some of the fish that you have just caught." So Simon Peter went aboard and hauled the net ashore, full of large fish, a hundred and fifty-three of them; and although there were so many, the net was not torn. Jesus said to them, "Come and have breakfast." Now none of the disciples dared ask him, "Who are you?" They knew it was the Lord. Jesus came and took the bread and gave it to them, and so with the fish. This was now the third time that Jesus was revealed to the disciples after he was raised from the dead.

When they had finished breakfast, Jesus said to Simon Peter, "Simon, son of John, do you love me more than these?" He said to him, "Yes, Lord; you know that I love you." He said to him, "Feed my lambs." A second time he said to him, "Simon, son of John, do you love me?" He said to him, "Yes, Lord; you know that I love you." He said to him, "Tend my sheep." He said to him the third time, "Simon, son of John, do you love me?" Peter was grieved because he said to him the third time, "Do you love me?" And he said to him, "Lord, you know everything; you know that I love you." Jesus said to him, "Feed my sheep. Truly, truly, I say to you, when you were young, you girded yourself and walked where you would; but when you are old, you will stretch out your hands, and another will gird you and carry you where you do not wish to go." (This he said to show by what death he was to glorify God.) And after this he said to him, "Follow me."

7

I Believe Jesus Goes On Before

The Sea of Life

"Some time later, Jesus showed himself to his disciples once again, by the Sea of Tiberias; and in this way. Simon Peter and Thomas 'the Twin' were together with Nathanael of Cana-in-Galilee. The sons of Zebedee and two other disciples were also there. Simon Peter said, 'I am going out fishing.' 'We will go with you', said the others. So they started and got into the boat. But that night they caught nothing.

"Morning came, and there stood Jesus on the beach, but the disciples did not know that it was Jesus. He called out to them, 'Friends, have you caught anything?' They answered 'No.' He said, 'Shoot the net to starboard, and you will make a catch.' They did so, and found they could not haul the net aboard, there were so many fish in it" (NEB).

The disciples had gone back home again. They had gone back to the place where Jesus had first asked them, "Follow me." They had gone back to their nets again. They had fished all night because that was the best time for fishing. They had had no luck. Now, morning was beginning to dawn. It was then that the stranger on the shore suggested that they cast their nets on the other side of the boat. They did so, and their nets were so full of fish that they could hardly get them ashore.

This was never meant to be seen as a miracle. It is rather an episode from everyday life. H. V. Morton describes a time when he saw two men fishing on the shores of a lake. One man had waded out from the shore and was casting a bell net into the water. He did it over and over again, but kept coming up empty. Then, a friend on the shore shouted to him to fling to the left. That time he was successful and the net was full of struggling fish. The man with the net had to rely on advice from the person on the shore. The man on the shore could see the shoal of fish in the clear water, while the man out in the water couldn't.

We don't have to have seen a sight like that or even be a fisherman to understand the experience of the disciples. In one way or another we have known what it is to toil in vain. We have had tasks that we have worked at and worked at and have wondered what we accomplished. We have had problems that we have fretted about day after day and wondered if we'd ever get them solved. We have had troubles that have weighed down our heart and we have wondered if we could keep giving of ourselves.

Some people have known, too, what it means to get help from a friend on the shore. We may have gone to a pastor for counseling. We may have sought advice from a friend or perhaps cried on his or her shoulder for awhile. We all have known what it means to be so close to a frustrating situation that we don't know which way to turn. How wonderful it is to have someone on the shore assisting us when we are fishing in vain.

Jesus came to the disciples when they needed him and showed them where to fish. The real blessing of the story is not that it happened once in Galilee, but that we can experience the same reality. In the midst of our work, our problems, our troubles, we can rely on the help of a friend on the shore of life. Jesus is calling to us as he called to the disciples. He asks us how we are doing. Are we finding what we are looking for? Is our life as meaningful and productive as it should be? If it isn't, he will tell us where we must turn. Then, we must turn to where he tells us. If we keep fishing in the same spot, we'll keep coming up with empty nets. We have to take his advice and do what he suggests, if we want our life to be full.

The Reality of the Resurrection

"That disciple whom Jesus loved said to Peter, "It is the Lord!" When Simon Peter heard that it was the Lord, he put on his clothes, for he was stripped for work, and sprang into the sea. But the other disciples came in the boat, dragging the net full of fish, for they were not far from the land, but about a hundred yards off.

When they got out on land, they saw a charcoal fire there, with fish lying on it, and bread. Jesus said to them, 'Bring some of the fish that you have just caught.' So Simon Peter went aboard and hauled the net ashore, full of large fish, a hundred and fifty-three of them; and although there were so many, the net was not torn. Jesus said to them, 'Come and have breakfast.' Now none of the disciples dared ask him, 'Who are you?' They knew it was the Lord. Jesus came and took the bread and gave it to them, and so with the fish. This was now the third time that Jesus was revealed to the disciples after he was raised from the dead."

We could look at Peter's action, diving into the water and wading ashore, in one of two different ways. We could see it from a positive point of view. We could see it as a wonderful thing that he did because he loved the Lord so much and wanted so much to come to him. We could praise Peter for what he did. We could also look at it the other way around and see it from a negative point of view. We could see it as a foolish action and a bit selfish. What he did seemed impressive, but it left the other disciples looking formal and cold. It left them with the task at hand to do, to come on in with the boat, towing the net full of fish.

Some of us are like Peter. Others are like the rest of the disciples. I suppose what we should gain from looking at them is that we need each other. We need those that are passionate in their feelings about Christ. We need those who express their devotion to Christ by doing the tasks that are at hand. Whatever is our nature, we need those who are opposite to give our discipleship the balance it needs to be healthy and creative.

They all came to Jesus. Peter by wading ashore; the others by rowing. Once on the shore, they had fellowship with Christ. He took bread and gave it to them and fish the same way. John wanted to make sure that those who would read his account of what happened wouldn't think that it was a figment of their imagination. He wanted everyone to know that Jesus really was there and that is why he told the story the way he did. In some ways, it sounds like Jesus appeared in a physical body. In other ways, it sounds like Jesus appeared in a spiritual body. Here, as in every case of his appearing after his resurrection, they at first didn't know who it was. I don't know if we can ever understand the mystery of it. I don't think it is that important. What is important is that we might know and respond to the presence of Christ in our lives. We might note that he appeared only to those that loved him. I think the same is true today.

We are told very simply that this was the third time that Jesus appeared to his disciples after his resurrection. Other events were of great meaning to them. Maundy Thursday was important. Jesus showed them by washing their feet that his disciples must be humble and that they should stop competing with each other. They shared in the Last Supper together, when Jesus told them that the bread he gave them was symbolic of his body and the cup symbolic of the blood he would shed for them and for us for the forgiveness of sins. The commandment he gave them that night was that they should love others as he loved them. That didn't empower them to take up the task he gave them. They couldn't even keep watch in the Garden when he prayed.

We talk about the power of the cross of Christ, and how, when we come to the cross, our lives will be changed. Let us be honest and realize that seeing Jesus suffer on the cross didn't change the disciples. They were still frightened and dismayed. Easter didn't empower them either. Christ had appeared to them in the Upper Room and they were overjoyed with the knowledge that he had conquered death and that he was risen indeed. He appeared to them a second time in the Upper Room, the time when Thomas was also there. They rejoiced together and believed in the resurrected Christ. Let's note what happened after that. They had been given the task of going out as servants of Christ into the world, but instead they had gone back home, back to their old tasks again.

How much like them we are! Many of us have had moments when we have gathered together in the fellowship of the church and we have felt the presence of Christ. We might have experienced it even more than once and known that the Resurrected Christ was with us. Then, what happened? Instead of taking up the task that he gave us, we have gone back home again, doing much the same old things as before.

This event, Christ's appearance on the shores of Galilee, enabled the disciples to accept the task Christ had given them so many times before. Christ had to appear to them as they were about their daily work. The same thing must happen to us. We must discover Jesus in our work-a-day world. We must find him present as we struggle with the common tasks of life. Only then, can we pick up the task he has given us over and over again—to serve others, to love others as he loves us. This story, then, is the heart of the gospel. Everything before was written in the light of it. Everything after was changed by it.

Mission Unlocks the Prison of Guilt

"When they had finished breakfast, Jesus said to Simon Peter, 'Simon, son of John do you love me more than these?' He said to him, 'Yes, Lord; you know that I love you.' He said to him, 'Feed my lambs.' A second time he said to him, 'Simon, son of John, do you love me?' He said to him, 'Yes, Lord; you know that I love you.' He said to him, 'Tend my sheep.' He said to him the third time, 'Simon, son of John, do you love me?' Peter was grieved because he said to him the third time, 'Do you love me?' And he said to him, 'Lord, you know everything; you know that I love you.' Jesus said to him, 'Feed my sheep. Truly, truly, I say to you, when you were young, you girded yourself and walked where you would; but when you are old, you will stretch out your hands, and another will gird you and carry you where you do not wish to go.' (This he said to show by what death he was to glorify God.) And after this he said to him, 'Follow me.' "

Peter didn't understand just what it was that Jesus was doing for him. He was hurt by the thing that finally set him free. Jesus knew Peter well. He knew his impetuous ways, his overeagerness, his overconfidence. More than that, he knew Peter's sense of guilt, his feeling of failure. He knew that Peter was immobilized by guilt. How many times Peter's mind must have gone back to the night of Jesus's arrest and trial. How many times he must have thought of how he denied Christ three times. How many times he must have hated himself for that. How many times he must have wished he could go back and live that night all over again.

Christ knew that this weighed heavily on his mind. Christ knew that he would have to be freed from the chain of guilt and failure if he was ever to be what Christ wanted him to be, if he was ever to do what Christ wanted him to do. If ever Peter was to be faithful, he had to feel redeemed of his faithlessness.

So Christ asked him three times if he loved him, once for each time that he had denied him. Each time Peter responded that he loved him, Christ asked him to feed his sheep. Peter knew then that he was forgiven. He also knew that if he really loved Christ, he would have to feed his sheep, he would have to serve other people at the point of their need. It wasn't enough just to tell Jesus that he loved him. He had to express that love he had for Christ by giving freely in love to others.

Peter came to leadership in the church on the other side of failure. I think we do too! He heard the call of Christ to follow him and he responded. Next, he denied Christ. Then, he discovered the risen Christ. Finally, he was sent in mission. Jesus lifted the weight of his guilt so that he wouldn't spend so much energy in regret and could spend it on loving others. There they were back on the shores of Galilee again. Christ said to Peter as he had at first, "Follow me."

Robert Raines has penned this prayer which I think we must make our own. "Set us free from what has been and what might have been to live for what may be. Give us a hope Lord and restore to me a future."

May the Lord set us free, not just so we won't feel so guilty about our sins and failures, but so that he might use us as he did Peter to do his great work.

Acts 3:1–16

Now Peter and John were going up to the temple at the hour of prayer, the ninth hour. And a man lame from birth was being carried, whom they laid daily at that gate of the temple which is called Beautiful to ask alms of those who entered the temple. Seeing Peter and John about to go into the temple, he asked for alms. And Peter directed his gaze at him, with John, and said, "Look at us." And he fixed his attention upon them, expecting to receive something from them. But Peter said, "I have no silver and gold, but I give you what I have; in the name of Jesus Christ of Nazareth, walk." And he took him by the right hand and raised him up; and immediately his feet and ankles were made strong. And leaping up he stood and walked and entered the temple with them, walking and leaping and praising God. And all the people saw him walking and praising God, and recognized him as the one who sat for alms at the Beautiful Gate of the temple; and they were filled with wonder and amazement at what had happened to him.

While he clung to Peter and John, all the people ran together to them in the portico called Solomon's, astounded. And when Peter saw it he addressed the people, "Men of Israel, why do you wonder at this, or why do you stare at us, as though by our own power or piety we had made him walk? The God of Abraham and of Isaac and of Jacob, the God of our fathers, glorified his servant Jesus, whom you delivered up and denied in the presence of Pilate, when he had decided to release him. But you denied the Holy and Righteous One, and asked for a murderer to be granted to you, and killed the Author of life, whom God raised from the dead. To this we are witnesses. And his name, by faith in his name, has made this man strong whom you see and know; and the faith which is through Jesus has given the man this perfect health in the presence of you all."

8

One Who Notices

He Was Carried

"Now Peter and John were going up to the temple at the hour of prayer, the ninth hour. And a man lame from birth was being carried, whom they laid daily by that gate of the temple called Beautiful to ask alms of those who entered the temple."

When we read the gospel stories, it is well that we put ourselves into the character in the account whenever that would fit. At first glance, very few of us, and perhaps very few people that we know, would relate to this crippled beggar that Peter and John met outside the temple. The man in the story was an individual that had to be carried by others. When we get this out of the arena of physical malady alone, all of a sudden the story applies to a great many people. He was a getter, not a giver. In other words, he needed the healing of Jesus Christ.

Dietrich Bonhoeffer has said, "In a Christian community everything depends upon whether each individual is an indispensable link in a chain. Only when even the smallest link is securely interlocked is the chain unbreakable. A community which allows unemployed members to exist within it will perish because of them. It will be well, therefore, if every member receives a definite task to perform for the community, that he may know in hours of doubt that he, too, is not useless and unusable. Every Christian community must realize that not only do the weak need the strong, but also that the strong cannot exist without the weak" (Dietrich Bonhoeffer, *Life Together* [New York: Harper & Row, 1954], p. 94).

We have allowed too many unemployed members to exist within the church. If Bonhoeffer is right, we will perish because of it. We have allowed too many persons to be carried by the giving of a few truly committed Christians.

How easy it is to admit that this is true and right away wonder why the pastors or someone else aren't doing more to involve these unemployed members. Since we are so quick to see our work as the responsibility of someone else, it is no wonder that it doesn't get done.

Carl Sandberg has written: "Who would want to go to a picnic all the time and eat out of other people's baskets? It is our obligation, as members of one church or another church, to give ourselves to it. It is the only hope of peace on earth and good will to men that exists among us. It is the church and its Savior, its Prince of Peace, who is the last hope of the earth, and yours is a high and holy opportunity to support it with your undeviating loyalty."

His imagery is biting. We know how we would feel if someone always came to every potluck with just plates and silverware, depending on others to provide the food or to do all the work. Yet, we have all allowed others to carry us as members of the church. To whatever extent that you are willing to see that this is true in your life, you need the healing power of Christ to transform you from a getter to a giver.

Peter Fixed His Eyes on Him

"When he saw Peter and John on their way into the temple he asked for charity. But Peter fixed his eyes on him, as John did also . . ." (NEB).

Peter and John fixed their eyes on the man. The man had been crippled from birth and was now past forty. Think of the number of people in those forty years that had walked by him and never noticed him. Others noticed that he was there but just treated him as a part of the landscape. Some must have given him handouts, and a lot of others must have patted their empty pockets. And still others didn't even make a pretense of concern. Peter and John were different, different because of having met Jesus and having committed themselves to him as their Lord. So they fixed their eyes on the man.

Someone has suggested that we could define a Christian as "one who notices." If you think about it, you will have to admit that it fits. A Christian is one who seeks to see things, who seeks to see people. A Christian is one who seeks to be sensitive to the sufferings of other persons. We won't always be as tuned in to others as we should. There are times when we won't hug the person that is feeling alone or cry with the person that is sad or walk a ways with the person that is afraid. Yet, we need to try as best we can, with what insight we have, with what strength we have, to be the people who see others.

Look At Us

"But Peter fixed his eyes on him, as John did also, and said, 'Look at us.' Expecting a gift from them, the man was all attention. And Peter said, 'I have no silver or gold; but what I have I give you: in the name of Jesus Christ of Nazareth, walk' " (NEB).

Peter said, "Look at us." We often want people to look at us. Children often say, "Look, mommy" or "Watch, daddy." As we get older, we often do the same thing, but with a little more subtlety. As both children and adults, what we are looking for is attention, praise, and recognition. In contrast, when the crippled beggar looked at Peter and John, he found that they were really looking at him and he saw in their eyes the love and compassion of Jesus Christ their Lord. Others had seen the beggar as a nuisance, a bag of bones, but Peter and John saw him as a person whom God loved and for whom Christ had died. Because they looked at him instead of at themselves, the man found healing.

Keith Miller tells the story about a busy New York executive who was struggling to live as a Christian day by day, but he was having a rather hard time of it. At least he was willing to deal with how he was falling short of the kind of life he knew that Christ wanted him to live, instead of taking the shortcut to feeling better by focusing on the failings of others. He made a resolution one particular morning that he would try to be a Christian in everything that happened that day. He was scheduled to leave from Grand Central Station by train for a business appointment in one of the suburbs. The traffic proved to be slow-moving and he was delayed in reaching the station. He arrived in time, however, to hear his train being called for departure. He quickly bought a ticket at the window and began to hurry down the ramp toward the train. In his haste, his briefcase struck a little child, knocking from his hands a box which contained a new jigsaw puzzle. The pieces went all over the place. The child began to cry.

The executive was caught up in an inner struggle: should he continue on ahead and catch the train or should he stop to help pick up the pieces of that puzzle. On the one hand, he reminded himself of just how important that appointment was and on the other hand, he couldn't block out the tear-flooded eyes of the boy. Finally, he smiled at the little boy and got down on his knees and began to pick up the pieces of the puzzle. As he was busy doing that, the train pulled out of the station. When the man handed the box back to the child, the little boy asked him, "Mister, are you Jesus?" He had indeed reflected the love of Christ in fixing his eyes on that boy (Keith Miller, *A Second Touch* [Waco, Texas: Word Books, 1967] pp. 63–64).

The church is meant to function as does the moon in relationship to the sun. The moon has no light of its own but reflects the light that the sun shines upon it. That is what Peter and John did for the crippled beggar. That is what the executive in New York City did for the boy with the scattered puzzle. That is what we are to do for each other, reflect the light of Christ in our daily living.

Notice how carefully Peter and John made the point that it was not through their own achievement that the man was healed, but through the power of Christ. We need to remember that. Our task is not to call attention to ourselves but to point people beyond us to the Lord we worship and serve. I hope that every night as you look up at the moon, it will serve as a daily reminder of your task as the church of Jesus Christ.

Peter told the cripple, "I have no silver or gold, but what I have I give you: in the name of Jesus Christ of Nazareth walk." How often we stop with the confession of what we don't have. We may say, "I don't have the talent," or "I don't have the time" or "I don't have the means." That usually boils down to, "I don't have the interest" or even more basically, "I don't have the love of Jesus Christ in my heart." Whenever we are focusing on what we don't have or what we think that we don't have, the work of the church, the work of Jesus Christ, just doesn't get done. When people look at us, they find us just looking at ourselves instead of looking at them. We need to move from focusing on what we don't have to give to what we do have to offer. Only then, will healing in the lives of people take place. Only then, will the church be the dynamic force in our lives and our community that it is meant to be. Only then will we be that body that reflects the light of the Son.

Acts 10:1—36

At Caesarea there was a man named Cornelius, a centurion of what was known as the Italian Cohort, a devout man who feared God with all his household, gave alms liberally to the people, and prayed constantly to God. About the ninth hour of the day he saw clearly in a vision an angel of God coming in and saying to him, "Cornelius." And he stared at him in terror, and said, "What is it, Lord? " And he said to him, "Your prayers and your alms have ascended as a memorial before God. And now send men to Joppa, and bring one Simon who is called Peter; he is lodging with Simon, a tanner, whose house is by the seaside." When the angel who spoke to him had departed, he called two of his servants and a devout soldier from among those that waited on him, and having related everything to them, he sent them to Joppa.

The next day, as they were on their journey and coming near the city, Peter went up on the housetop to pray, about the sixth hour. And he became hungry and desired something to eat; but while they were preparing it, he fell into a trance and saw the heaven opened, and something descending, like a great sheet, let down by four corners upon the earth. In it were all kinds of animals and reptiles and birds of the air. And there came a voice to him, "Rise, Peter; kill and eat." But Peter said "No, Lord; for I have never eaten anything that is common or unclean." And the voice came to him again a second time, "What God has cleansed, you must not call common." This happened three times, and the thing was taken up at once to heaven.

Now while Peter was inwardly perplexed as to what the vision which he had seen might mean, behold, the men that were sent by Cornelius, having made inquiry for Simon's house, stood before the gate and called out to ask whether Simon who was called Peter was lodging there. And while Peter was pondering the vision, the Spirit said to him, "Behold, three men are looking for you. Rise and go down, and accompany them without hesitation; for I have sent them." And Peter went down to the men and said, "I am the one you are looking for; what is the reason for your coming?" And they said, "Cornelius, a centurion, an upright and God-fearing man, who is well spoken of by the whole Jewish nation, was directed by a holy angel to send for you to come to his house, and to hear what you have to say." So he called them in to be his guests.

The next day he rose and went off with them, and some of the brethren from Joppa accompanied him. And on the following day they entered Caesarea. Cornelius was expecting them and had called together his kinsmen and close friends. When Peter entered, Cornelius met him and fell down at his feet and worshiped him. But Peter lifted him up, saying, "Stand up; I too am a man." And as he talked with him, he went in and found many persons gathered; and he said to them, "You yourselves know how unlawful it is for a Jew to associate with or to visit any one of another nation; but God has shown me that I should not call any man common or unclean. So when I was sent for, I came without objection. I ask then why you sent for me."

And Cornelius, said, "Four days ago, about this hour, I was keeping the ninth hour of prayer in my house; and behold, a man stood before me in bright apparel, saying, 'Cornelius, your prayer has been heard and your alms have been remembered before God. Send therefore to Joppa and ask for Simon who is called Peter; he is lodging in the house of Simon, a tanner, by the seaside.' So I sent to you at once, and you have been kind enough to come. Now therefore we are all here present in the sight of God, to hear all that you have been commanded by the Lord."

And Peter opened his mouth and said: "Truly I perceive that God shows no partiality, but in every nation any one who fears him and does what is right is acceptable to him. You know the word which he sent to Israel, preaching good news of peace by Jesus Christ (he is Lord of all)."

9

God Has No Favorites

In the earliest days of the church, it was taken for granted by the leaders of the Christian movement that a person had to become a Jew prior to becoming a Christian. Christianity was a kind of branch or expression of Judaism. Then, there came the moment of decision whether Christianity would be confined within the boundaries of Judaism or not. It was God's will that his revelation in Jesus Christ would be not only something for the Jew but the Gentile as well. To accomplish his will, God brought together two men who in many respects were very different from each other. When they came together, it was a time of interface, not only for them as individuals, but for the whole church.

Cornelius Changed His Mind About God

Cornelius was a Roman, a leader of a cohort of six hundred soldiers. The Scriptures describe him as a religious man, though he had not become a Jew. He was a Gentile who came regularly to the Jewish worship services, contributed generously, and was regular in his prayers to God. Though these good things are recognized of him, a strict Jew would have had no contact with him because he was a Gentile and because he did not observe the Law.

God spoke to Cornelius in a very personal way and directed him to invite Peter to his home. He sent the invitation to Peter, and Peter came and told Cornelius the good news of Jesus Christ. We are told that the Holy Spirit came upon them as they heard Peter preach the message of salvation. Then Peter spoke: " 'Is anyone prepared to withhold the water for baptism from these persons, who have received the Holy Spirit just as we did ourselves?' Then he ordered them to be baptized in the name of Jesus Christ."

Cornelius needed Peter to help him change his mind about God. He had a commitment to religion in general, to doing good and to praying regularly. However, he needed God's revelation through Peter in order to come to a real commitment to Jesus Christ as his Lord and Savior. As Peter preached, God touched Cornelius and he responded and was baptized as a disciple of Christ.

I once had the opportunity of studying in Switzerland, under Dr. Paul Tournier, a Christian medical doctor. There is a radiance that comes from that man that can be experienced, but not easily described. Little did I know until I met him that he had been an orphan who had had great difficulty being accepted and accepting himself. The first significant step towards acceptance and self-acceptance was made possible by the interest which his Greek professor took in him. The professor was not a religious man, but invited the lonely young Paul into his home and into his intellectual world. Dr. Tournier said, "He reinserted me back into humanity." Many years later, long after Dr. Tournier had become a Christian, he cast about in his mind for some friend who might read and offer suggestions on his first manuscript before it went to the printer. His thoughts went back of his old Greek professor, now retired.

After having asked his professor to look at the manuscript, and the professor having agreed to do so, he then asked Dr. Tournier to read the first chapter to him. When the chapter was completed and Dr. Tournier looked up for a critical reaction, the old man said merely, "Paul, continue." He read another chapter. "Paul, continue." He read the third chapter. Then, the old teacher, said, "Paul, we must pray together." They prayed. Afterward, Dr. Tournier exclaimed, "But I didn't know you were a Christian." "Yes." "When did you become a Christian?" "Just now."

There is no set way, no set place, no set method by which one becomes a Christian. Like Cornelius and this professor, there are many who have to move from a general respect for God, to real commitment to God by accepting Jesus Christ as Lord. Some of you may be Cornelius in some way or another. God may be trying to reach through to you, hoping that you will respond with faith as Cornelius did.

Peter Changed His Mind About People

While Cornelius had to change his mind about God, Peter had to change his mind about people. We can see that he was struggling with whether to take literally the laws of the Old Testament or not. By the mere fact that he was staying with Simon the tanner in Joppa, he was going against what is written in Numbers 19:11–13. Since a tanner worked with the bodies of dead animals, he was considered unclean. Peter's vision on the roof top was a struggle within himself whether or not to take literally the stringent food regulations of the Old Testament. We find these in Leviticus 11. Peter heard a voice which said to him, "Up, Peter, kill and eat." It is no wonder that Peter protested because the voice was telling him not to take literally words of Scripture that he had held dear and observed faithfully. "The voice came again a second time: 'It is not for you to call profane what God counts clean.' This happened three times; and then the thing was taken up again into the sky" (NEB). The voice he heard was the Holy Spirit.

The message of this passage is very clear and very direct. It says to us that when Jesus Christ truly lives in you, he helps you take down barriers. For Peter, that meant not only coming to a new attitude toward the Gentiles, but also that he had to have a new attitude toward the Scriptures if he was going to be faithful to the Holy Spirit.

Dr. William Stidger, the great preacher and professor at Boston University, once visited a mission station in Northern Luzon of the Philippines. Accompanied by photographers, the mission group made one of the first visits by outsiders to a particular tribe of the Negritos people. The missionaries arrived in the village at noon time and proceeded to eat their lunch with the pygmy-like Negritos gathered quietly around them. The missionaries could not help but comment on the squalor of the natives, especially one old man, more repulsive than the rest, with sores on his face and hands.

"That one is about as close to an animal as any being I have ever seen," remarked one of the missionaries. "You are right," Stidger agreed. "He reminds me of an orangutan, except that he is smaller."

"I've seen most of the wild tribes in existence today," said a photographer, "but I have never seen anyone as low on the human scale." It was decided that whatever scraps were left from lunch would be given to the old man just to see what would happen, for he did seem to be the leader of the tribe.

Imagine the chagrin of those "civilized" missionaries of Jesus Christ when the old man took not one bit for himself but divided up the leftovers among his people, making sure that every person, young and old, had an equal share. Dr. Stidger was feeling somewhat ill from the heat, and the old man, having sensed this, had water brought from a nearby spring. William Stidger ends his telling of the incident by saying that he knew he was hypocritical at times, but never was he more sure of it than that day when he received a cup of water from a little Negritos in a Luzon jungle and remembered the words: "When I was thirsty ye gave me to drink . . . When I was a stranger ye took me in." Dr. Stidger thought that he was the one representing Christ to the Negritos. He found out how hypocritical he was and how much the old man understood the message of Christ, though he had not yet called him, "Lord."

Peter was struggling with his relationship to people, too. It involved some old prejudices that the Jews were right and the Gentiles were not. It involved some old prejudices that God cared especially for the Jews and not so much for the Gentiles because they did not have the faith of Abraham. Some of you may be like Peter, in one way or another. God may be trying to reach through to you, hoping that you will respond with faith as Peter did, to become more accepting of others.

God Does Not Have Favorites

Peter began his message to Cornelius: "I now see how true it is that God has no favorites, but that in every nation the man who is godfearing and does what is right is acceptable to him" (NEB). For Peter, that struggle involved whether the Jews were more favored in God's eyes than the Gentiles. In our day, the struggle may be between the conservative and liberal Christian. God has no favorites. God doesn't love fundamentalists more than liberals or Methodists more than Baptists. God loves us all equally with a love greater than we can comprehend. God wants of us a love for each other that reflects the love he has for us.

There is no question that God brought Cornelius and Peter together. God brought them together because they needed each other in order to understand the fullness of God. They were very different so it was not easy. It was a struggle, particularly for Peter. He went back to the church in Jerusalem feeling that God had led him to a new understanding of his Will. When the leaders of the early Christian church found out that Peter had baptized a Gentile who had not first been circumcised they were very alarmed. This was the main cause for their anger. So they brought charges against Peter for breaking the Law. Having simply entered the house of a Gentile and eaten a meal with him, Peter had broken the Law handed down to Moses.

Peter was God's spokesman in seeking to tear down the barriers between believers who were Jews and those who were Gentiles. Even Peter, though, backed away from the truth that God had showed him and, for a time, yielded to the pressures of the circumcision party. Then, in Antioch, Peter was confronted by Paul and challenged to have the courage to live out his convictions even under fire.

We often live out that same drama in our own lives. God reveals his truth to us and we seek to follow it. Then, when we begin to implement it, often there are difficulties and pressures that arise. We may very well back off from what we know we should do, just as Peter did. God reaches out to us time and again seeking to bring us back to what is true and right. We need constantly to be reminded that God has no favorites.

Acts 12:1-17

About that time Herod the king laid violent hands upon some who belonged to the church. He killed James the brother of John with the sword; and when he saw that it pleased the Jews, he proceeded to arrest Peter also. This was during the days of Unleavened Bread. And when he had seized him, he put him in prison, and delivered him to four squads of soldiers to guard him, intending after the Passover to bring him out to the people. So Peter was kept in prison; but earnest prayer for him was made to God by the church.

The very night when Herod was about to bring him out, Peter was sleeping between two soldiers, bound with two chains, and sentries before the door were guarding the prison; and behold, an angel of the Lord appeared, and a light shone in the cell; and he struck Peter on the side and woke him, saying, "Get up quickly." And the chains fell off his hands. And the angel said to him, "Dress yourself and put on your sandals." And he did so. And he said to him, "Wrap your mantle around you and follow me." And he went out and followed him; he did not know that what was done by the angel was real, but thought he was seeing a vision. When they had passed the first and the second guard, they came to the iron gate leading into the city. It opened to them of its own accord, and they went out and passed on through one street; and immediately the angel left him. And Peter came to himself, and said, "Now I am sure that the Lord has sent his angel and rescued me from the hand of Herod and from all that the Jewish people were expecting."

When he realized this, he went to the house of Mary, the mother of John whose other name was Mark, where many were gathered together and were praying. And when he knocked at the door of the gateway, a maid named Rhoda came to answer. Recognizing Peter's voice, in her joy she did not open the gate but ran in and told that Peter was standing at the gate. They said to her, "You are mad." But she insisted that it was so. They said, "It is his angel!" But Peter continued knocking; and when they opened, they saw him and were amazed. But motioning to them with his hand to be silent, he described to them how the Lord had brought him out of the prison. And he said, "Tell this to James and to the brethren." Then he departed and went to another place.

10

One Street Farther

The Appearance

"On the night before Herod was going to bring him into court, Peter, fettered with two chains, was sleeping between two soldiers, and the guards, stationed in front of the door, were keeping watch over the prison. An angel of the Lord appeared, and a light shone in the building. The angel touched Peter's side, and wakened him. 'Quick!' he said. 'Up!' His fetters fell from his hands. 'Fasten your belt,' the angel said, 'and put on your sandals.' Peter did so. 'Put on your coat,' the angel said, 'and follow me.' So he went out and followed him. He did not realize that what was being done by the angel was really happening; he thought that he was seeing a vision. They passed through the first and second guards, and came to the iron gate which led into the city. All by itself it opened for them" (Barclay).

Much that is in this account is frankly beyond our comprehension. It is good that we recognize and appreciate that there is much about life and much about how God works that we cannot fully understand.

Certainly, all the elements are there to see it as a miracle. Verse upon verse relates how things happened that defy logical explanation. Beneath it all is the affirmation made by the early Church that it was God through the angel that rescued Peter from prison. We cling to the miraculous aspect of this story and others, because we so often face situations for which we see no answer or no solution. It is strengthening to believe that God can act to bring about changes in circumstances in which we see simply no way out.

Others who believe just as thoroughly in God and in the Scriptures may stress how God has set up laws and principles in the universe. While we may not understand them all, God works through the dependable operation of the laws of life. It is interesting that William Barclay, the great New Testament scholar and evangelical says: "In this story we do not necessarily need to see a miracle. It may well be the story of a thrilling rescue and escape. Even if it were such, it would still have been told in the same terms because, however it happened, the hand of God was most definitely in it."

Why would someone just not want to see it as a miracle? Why would anyone want to question in any way the miraculous way in which God acted and acts? I think, more often than not, it is not out of a sense of unbelief but out of a sense of appreciation. More often than not, God does not get us out of our troubles, but rather sees us through them. The supreme example, of course, is that God did not send his angels to get Jesus down from the cross. Instead, he gave Jesus the strength to bear the cross.

We often pray for God's intervention. If what we pray for doesn't happen, it does not mean that God has forsaken us. When a cross cannot be removed, God will help us to bear it if we turn to him for the strength and love he offers.

I often anticipate problems. Sometimes that is good. Hopefully, you can figure out solutions ahead of time to the problems that you could not think through fast enough or well enough just at the time. That quality may have saved me from some grief, but more often than not, it has brought grief. You can worry and fret about problems that never arise and this saps your strength. Worrying about something can often help to enhance its possibilities of happening. That is why I like the fact that as Peter came to the iron gate it opened all by itself. That which in anticipation would have been an insurmountable problem didn't prove to be a problem at all. Each detail of the story bears that out. That speaks a needed word to me and perhaps to you. The troubles, the difficulties that stagger us in anticipation begin to shrink when they are faced, when they are shouldered. If we trust in God and do what he asks of us, as did Peter, the simple fact is that iron gates will open.

The great Houdini, a master magician as well as a fabulous locksmith, bragged that he could escape from any jail cell in the world in less than an hour, provided he could go into the cell dressed in his street clothes. A small town in the British Isles built a new jail, of which they were extremely proud, and issued Houdini a challenge. "Come give us a try," they said. Houdini loved the publicity, so he accepted the city's challenge. By the time Houdini arrived, excitement was at its peak. He rode triumphantly into town and walked into the cell. Confidence oozed from him as the door was closed. Hidden in his belt was a flexible, tough, and durable ten-inch piece of steel which he used to work on the lock. At the end of thirty minutes, his confidence had disappeared. At the end of an hour, he was drenched in perspiration, and after two hours, Houdini literally collapsed against the door—which opened! The jail door had never been locked except in Houdini's own mind, which made it as firmly locked as if hundreds of locksmiths had put their best locks on it.

Can you see yourself in that story? So many people are imprisoned behind doors that are already unlocked. Sometimes the harder we struggle to get out by our own craftiness or ingenuity, the more our confidence in ourselves and our strength is drained. The jail doors in our life are locked only in our own mind. God has unlocked them in the life and death of Jesus Christ. If we trust him, if we obey him, and walk with him toward the freedom he has promised, they will open one by one.

The Departure

"They went out, and they went one street farther, and then suddenly the angel left him" (Barclay).

I think that our temptation in reading this story is to focus on the appearance of the angel, and what happened as a result, and forget about the departure of the angel. The symbolism is so powerful that it is almost overwhelming. The angel guided Peter out of prison and went one street farther. Then, the angel left. It didn't mean that he was then alone. God was still with Peter. You see, there came a place where God had to let go, and leave what was going to happen next up to Peter.

Peter didn't fall apart when the angel left him. He kept on going. That is what we are to do. He sought out his brothers and sisters in the faith. That is what we are to do.

A cold wind howled and rain beat down when the telephone rang in a country doctor's house. "It's my wife," a voice said. "She needs a doctor right away." "Can you come and get me?" the physician asked, "My car's being repaired." "What?" came the sputtering reply. "Go out in this weather?"

I like that story because it brings humor which heals to pain that I have felt at times. People are often quick to ask you to render a service, but it is a different thing when the same is asked of them. When you think about it, you realize that we often do the very same thing with God. We call upon him for help, and want his response to the need, but when something is asked of us, even to fulfill what we seem to want to happen, we give a sputtering reply.

I like the fact, built into the heart of life itself, that God will guide us out of prison, will walk with us one street farther, and then it is up to us.

Failure to Believe

"Peter knocked at the door of the gateway, and a maidservant called Rhoda came to answer his knock. She recognized Peter's voice, and she was so overcome with joy that, instead of opening the gate, she ran in with the news that Peter was standing at the gate. 'You're raving,' they said to her. She insisted that he was there. 'It is his angel,' they said. Peter went on knocking. When they opened the door, they were astonished to see him" (Barclay).

They had been fervently praying for Peter's release. Their prayers were answered and Peter was at the door. They were slow to believe that God had done what they had asked him to do. They had gone through all the right motions. They had come together in fellowship. They had prayed. Yet, the quality of real trust, real belief that God was hearing their prayers and would respond was not as strong as it should be. God did answer their prayers but they were slow to see and believe in his answer. How like them we are all too often. We go through all the right motions but our quality of trust in God's answer is not what it should be.

I'm glad that Peter kept on knocking. That shows another side of Peter that we usually don't see. He was usually fiery, impulsive, passionate. Here he showed the quality of persistence. You know, there is always another side to the character of others if we will take the time to see it. There is always another side to our own character if we will make the effort with God's help to develop it.

Peter's persistence in knocking at the door is like the patience of God. God is knocking at the door of our life. If in faith we will open that door, God will surely be there.

SYMBOLS

THE SEAL OF ST. PETER. Peter felt unworthy to die as had Christ, so he requested that his cross be inverted so that he could look heavenward as he was dying. The crossed keys symbolize the Keys of the Kingdom of Heaven.

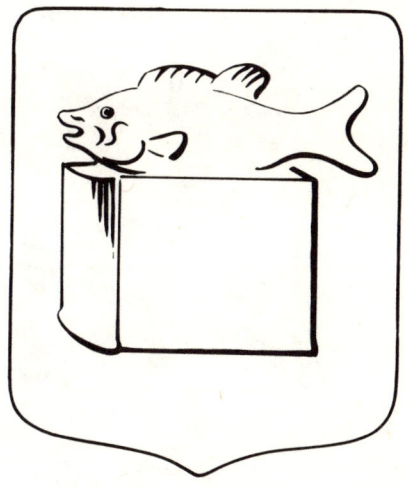

THE FISH AND THE BIBLE. Simon Peter was known as a great fisher of men through the power of the gospel.

THE COCK recalls Jesus' words to Peter "...this night before the cock crows twice, you will deny me three times." The cock on the weather-vane on church steeples faces us with a watchful warning and a constant reminder of Jesus' words.

THE ROCK. "Built on a rock the church doth stand..." A symbol of Jesus' words to Peter "...on this rock I will build my church."

PETER'S CROSS